1 85103 044 1

First published 1986 by Editions Gallimard
First published 1988 in Great Britain by Moonlight Publishing Ltd,
131 Kensington Church Street, London W8
© 1986 by Editions Gallimard
English text © 1988 by Moonlight Publishing Ltd

Printed in Italy by Editoriale Libraria

CLOTHES
THROUGH THE AGES
A HISTORY OF COSTUME: VOL 1

DISCOVERERS

Written and illustrated by
Jean-Louis Besson

Translated by Sarah Matthews

MOONLIGHT PUBLISHING

Contents

The Stone Age was tens of thousands of years ago. The weather had become a lot colder since earlier times when Europe had a warm, tropical climate, and people walked around rather more decorated than dressed.

The Bronze Age: woven, sleeved top and fringed skirt. Woven belt decorated with metal disc.

Elephants, rhinoceros and hippopotami had made way for reindeer, bears and lions. Their skins, sewn together with hair or sinews, made excellent, warm clothing.

Skins from the legs made braces or belts, and the tails hung down at the backs of the skirts.

For jewellery, people used animal teeth and bones, stones and pieces of amber.

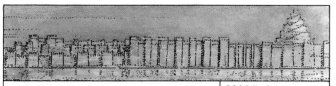

At Sumer, in Mesopotamia, they didn't wear animal skins around their shoulders, but fastened them like skirts around their hips. These garments, made of hairy goat or sheep skins, or, later on, of cloth woven to imitate the same effect, were called kaunakès. They remained popular right up until the Middle Ages.

Later on, in Babylon, people wore long woollen shawls, often draped over a short-sleeved tunic. Both shawls and tunics had long fringes and were dyed bright colours, particularly red. The men oiled and curled their beards and their hair, even when they wore wigs.

The King of Ur wore a sheepskin skirt or kaunakès.

Leather sandals protected Babylonian feet from the sun-baked paving stones.

9

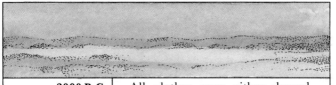

2000 B.C.

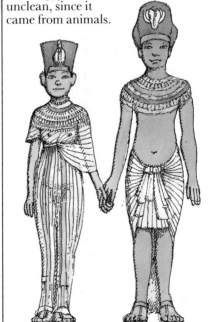

All clothes were either draped – wrapped round the body and fixed with pins or a belt – or else sewn – cut to fit the body, arms and legs.

The nomads of the Mongolian steppes wore sewn clothes. They were the first people to wear trousers.

The **Egyptians**, like all the Mediterranean peoples, preferred draped clothing. Most of their clothes were made of linen, which came from plants and was naturally white, because the Egyptians believed wool was unclean, since it came from animals.

Scythians and Huns swept westward into Europe in their goat-skin cloaks and the trousers that made horse-riding so much easier and more comfortable.

Nefertiti and her husband, the pharaoh Akhenaton. Her gown is of linen woven so finely that it is almost transparent.

10

Linen made cool, transparent clothing, which hung in fine folds. Rich women would wear tiny coronets of gold wire perched on top of the wigs which they put over their own hair. Dancing girls, who were slaves, wore nothing but a belt round their waists—those with the least wore the least.

The men often shaved their skulls and wore wigs only on feast-days.

1500 B.C.

The Egyptians loved white, and rather despised the gaudy, multicoloured clothes of their neighbours the Libyans, Syrians, Phoenicians and Hebrews.

Three and a half thousand years ago, the merchants of **Crete** were masters of the Aegean Sea from Greece to the Cyclades. People on Crete behaved like nobody else in the Mediterranean world: ordinary women were allowed out of the house to take part in business! The women's clothes were distinctive too. They were the only clothes in the Mediterranean to be cut and sewn. A tight-fitting blouse was nipped in at the waist and curved round to display the naked breasts, while the skirts were flounced out in several layers.

Cretan men were more simply dressed, with two or three tunics one on top of the other.

Skirts and bodices were reinforced with cane, and sometimes even with copper. The royal ladies of the palace of Knossos had their feet rouged. They never walked out of doors.

The Cretans were finely dressed and had a great reputation for curiosity. Wherever they travelled, they brought back items of interest and beauty to their island home.

The clothes **the Greeks** wore were made up of different-sized rectangles of wool or linen, held together on the shoulders by two brooches or fibula and by a belt at the waist.

The women wrapped themselves in a peplos two metres long and a metre and a half wide. Or they would wear a chiton, which was smaller and sewn into a tube shape. Boys wore chitons, too, as tunics.

The chlamys was a short cloak, fastened with a clasp at the shoulder. Another kind of cloak, the hymation, was two metres long and could be used as a blanket at night. One accessory was important: the ribbon or scarf tied round the hair.

800 B.C.

Athletes competed naked.

The same length of cloth could serve as clothing for both men and women. The story goes that Phocion, a disgraced general, was so poor that he and his wife had but the one piece of cloth between them. If one of them went out, the other was left at home naked . . .

13

750 B.C.

The Etruscans picked up fashions from everywhere: a Greek chiton underneath an Oriental shawl.

When Romulus and Remus, the two founders of **Rome**, were being suckled by the she-wolf who had adopted them, the Etruscans had already transformed the Greek rectangle into a draped semi-circle.

This semi-circle became the Roman toga. It was so big – up to seven metres wide – and so heavy that the wearer had to have help putting it on. The law was very definite about what men could wear: magistrates wore white, triumphant generals wore purple and gold. Women, however, could wear any colour they liked.

On ceremonial occasions, the toga was draped over the head.

Social life was very important to the Romans, and going to the baths was an important part of that. Men and women spent hours bathing and attending to their appearance. Women who couldn't spend their time, as Poppea did, soaking every day in the milk of five hundred asses, would make face-masks of bread-crumbs soaked in milk, and then put on a lotion made from pressed flowers.

300 B.C.

The aquatic dancers of the Piazza Armerina in Sicily wore two-piece bathing-suits.

On the other side of the Alps, **the Celts** were already well known for the quality of their clothing and jewels.

When Julius Caesar's soldiers occupied Gaul, they were very taken by the trousers which the Scythians had imported and which the Gauls now wore. They became so fashionable that the traditionalist Emperor Diocletian passed a law, forbidding their being worn in Rome.

15

AD 400

However savage their reputation, **the Goths, the Huns and the Saxons** were brilliant craftsmen – gold, bronze and copper took on an elaborate and animated life in their hands.

Europe was invaded by barbarians. They wore horned helmets, plaits and fitted tunics. They even sometimes wore tunics made of chain-mail. They were highly skilled metal-workers.

During this time, two monks returned to Byzantium from China. Underneath their robes, which marked them as holy men so that they were not searched at the customs, they smuggled two silk-worm cocoons – and with them the secret of silk-making.

Silk completely changed the appearance of clothes. It was too light to be draped, and too expensive to wear in bulk. But what was lost in extent was more than made up for in the richness of decoration and jewellery.

Byzantine dress was highly luxurious. It made use of all sorts of different styles, from the Persians to the Graeco-Roman West. The ancient toga became a cloak woven with gold, worn over a tunic encrusted with pearls and embroidery. Narrow trousers were decorated with embroidered flowers. For women, a long veil shaded the head.

Byzantine silk embroidery: four horses pulling a cart

Ostrogoth brooch: bird of prey in *cloisonné* bronze

The Normans in the last of the great invasions, brought to Europe all the skills of the Vikings. They made brooches shaped like interlocking serpents, or like dragons.

The Merovingians and the Carolingians wore a short tunic, the gonelle, which was practical for horseback-riding. But people still wore long robes as well.

Beneath a Roman cloak, a loose gonelle fastened with a low-slung belt. Cross-gartering ran up from soft leather shoes.

A long tunic with a full pallium over it

Belts were important because these clothes had no pockets. Everything – money, scissors, a comb – had to be carried in a pouch hanging from the belt.

Golden earring fit for a queen

Men and women often dressed in the same way. The Pope Agathon was worried about this, because he was well aware of the mistakes which could arise. Some people wore a long linen tunic, with narrow sleeves which tightened at the wrist, while others preferred a short tunic with long, trailing sleeves.

Fancy effects: a left sleeve twice as heavily decorated as the right

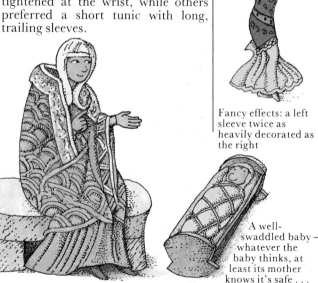

A well-swaddled baby – whatever the baby thinks, at least its mother knows it's safe . . .

1100

Crusaders, exhausted after their long journey to the East, rediscovered a fabled land of wealth and beauty: silk robes embroidered with pearls, turbans dyed in fantastic colours, cloaks made of ermine or of white fox carried by trading caravans from afar.

Pilgrims wore a wide-brimmed hat decorated with a scallop-shell picked up on the beach near the shrine of St James of Compostella.

During the Middle Ages, poor people all wore very similar clothes. Peasants usually wore a short tunic. A shepherd wore leggings and a hood covering his head and shoulders. The monk's long, hooded robe was also worn by people working in the country. These medieval working clothes are still the model for monks' and nuns' wear today.

1250

Not everyone took part in the festivities on All Fools' Day. The rich would simply sit and watch. Rich women's sleeves were so tight that they had to be unpicked every night and sewn up again in the mornings. Undressing quickly, without help, was not the mark of a virtuous woman.

The church ordained that Jews should wear a distinguishing mark: a tall pointed yellow hat.

For him, a light coronet; for her, a delicate crown

His and hers fur-lined cloaks

Power began to shift away from the great lords. Trades organized themselves into guilds. For artists, a new idea: the search for beauty.

1350. Men's tunics were short. Both men's and women's clothes were fitted, buttoned and laced. Styles became more fantastic and extravagant: fashion had been born.

At the doctor's, the patient lifts his tunic to reveal hose fastened to his belt with laces, or points.

Hats, particularly women's hats, became extraordinary constructions of fabric and stuffing and pins. The Church saw these horned hats as being the work of the devil, and one monk, Thomas, gave sermons telling children to run after women wearing these hats and shout at them. The name 'hennin', which probably started as an insult, stuck.

AU HENNIN AU HENNIN !

Men wore a cap set high on the head. The short, quilted tunics they wore meant that stockings came higher up, fitting closely to the leg and fastened at the top with a triangle which developed in time into the cod-piece. Women had tight bodices with a belt high up just below the breasts. Under their dresses they wore little padded bags giving them the round-bellied shape so fashionable at the time. The houppelande soon became all the rage. It was sewn in folds and the long sleeves were often scalloped and trimmed.

1400

Bath-houses were popular.

1450. In France, there was the Hundred Years' War, in England, the Wars of the Roses. **In Italy,** there were the early stirrings of the Renaissance. On feast-days people would be 'disguised' – not dressed in the 'ordinary guise' of every day.

The women wore embroidered houppelandes over tight bodices, while men had hats with long scarves wound round them. They had short surcoats or paletots, which slipped on over the head. Particoloured hose gave them brilliant, unmatching legs.

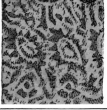

1470

In Venice, the gondoliers had ostrich or peacock feathers stuck in their caps, and striped tights decorating their legs.

Here, the silk trade with the East had never been interrupted. It formed the basis for the amazing velvets woven by the Venetian craftsmen.

The Doge, ruler of Venice, wore a hat with a point at the back. Venetian women had buns high on their heads. They started the fashion for special scraps of cloth for wiping nose and eyes: handkerchiefs.

The invention of the printing press: first came the Bible, but fashion plates weren't far behind

A rich young man sporting a red velvet cap and a peacock feather

Everywhere else in Europe people had to have their hairline plucked to show off their high, white brows. The women wore a light scarf rolled round their high buns, or a hat of fine cloth shaped round a wicker frame, or black velvet ribbons emphasizing their pale skins, or hats of black velvet surrounding their faces. Low-cut necklines began their career downwards.

Christopher Columbus offered a prize of 10,000 gold pieces a year and a suit of red velvet for the first man to sight land.

At the court of Castille, Queen Juanita of Portugal had pressing reasons for hiding the fact that she was pregnant – her husband had long been an invalid ... She set the fashion for the farthingale – a skirt draped over ever-wider wicker hoops.

Another fashion was for slashed sleeves, which let the undershirt show through as it poked out of the holes.

Gradually, the Renaissance was beginning to change things all over Europe. New trends were for smooth lines, low necklines, full sleeves, and, for the men, flat hats decorated with feathers.

In England, men wore pointed hats, like the one Robin Hood wore in Sherwood Forest. They had doga-lines, sleeveless coats imported from Venice.

In France, even the men went in for low-cut necklines. The sleeves of their tunics and coats were padded almost to splitting point. Hose were now of two kinds: long breeches, joined at the front by a prominent cod-piece, which could be used as a pocket, since there were still no pockets in the clothes, or tightly woven stockings made of silk.

The shoes were flat, with square toes.

For all the finery, the Renaissance was marked as a time when perfume had to do battle with body odour. The difficulty of cleaning the heavy clothes and the new prudishness imposed by the Reformation both combined to banish the personal cleanliness of the Middle Ages.

1540

Still cosily swaddled, babies were saved from the temptation of sucking their thumbs.

After the Battle of Pavia, Spanish stiffness won the day. No more low necklines; dresses were now pyramid-shaped, with high collars and padded shoulders. Black and gold were the dominant colours. Men wore their swords at their sides.

Venice, though, stayed immune from Spanish influence. There, women walked about on clogs with thirty-centimetre high heels. Some of them even dared to wear breeches under their skirts ... How to become a Venetian blond: wear a hat without a crown. Your hair will be bleached by the sun, while your skin still keeps its desirable pallor.

Queen Elizabeth I of England owned six thousand dresses and over sixty wigs. She loved ruffs.

Women's farthingales became wider and wider, while men started wearing padded tunics to protect themselves from stab-wounds. Round their necks they wore high, starched, tightly folded ruffs. Breeches could be very short or could go down to just below the knee. A round hat worn on the back of the head was called a polonaise.

Queen Elizabeth
in court dress

1630

While the countries of Europe fought each other for supremacy, France quietly took over the fashion lead.

Some people in Holland stayed faithful to the millstone ruff – stiff, starched ruffs made bigger than ever before. But clothes, like the arts, sciences and philosophy, were undergoing radical transformations in this century of change.

English Puritan women covered their hair with white bonnets and high black hats. It was a fashion taken to America by the first English settlers.

Lord Denbigh, returning from India, introduced braces as worn by the Moguls, with a loose floating jacket over the top.

Gone was the farthingale. Women regained their natural shape. Their faces were framed with fringes curled *en garcette*. They wore three dresses, one over the other: a gown decorated with ribbons and frills opening over an underskirt, and, underneath it all, a shift.

Men wore wide-brimmed, plumed felt hats, and wore their jackets slung over one shoulder. Ruffs gave way to a lace collar or falling band. Men wore high, floppy boots with the tops turned out, or shoes decorated with bunches of ribbons.

Some clothes clearly advertized the wearer's role in life.

Girls were never allowed out unaccompanied. Their chaperones, or duennas, with their elaborately decorated hats, made sure that they didn't get up to anything that would damage their reputations – and their value on the marriage-market.

Doctor

Nun

Priest

Judge

Nuns simply wore the ordinary clothes of poor working women. But men in high office, whether teachers, lawyers or priests, wore long robes of black or red cloth, or, best of all, hemmed with ermine, to show how grand they were.

Water-seller

Vinegar-seller

Street-traders sang songs about their wares to attract customers as they strolled along.

Street musician

Pieman

Actors wore flat-topped hats and multicoloured suits adapted from the motley worn by court fools in the Middle Ages.

Street traders needed clothes that could be kept clean and which made it possible to move about easily. A pheasant feather in the cap was a cheap and easily replaced decoration.

The Spanish, having changed their farthingales for gardinfantas, which were wider but still very stiff, found at Versailles the new fashion thought up by the young Louis XIV. There were ribbons, feathers and lace frothing everywhere. The pourpoint had become a brassière, with the shirt puff-

ing out at sleeves and neck. The most extraordinary item of all was the rhinegrave, short, wide, heavily pleated trousers, hung about with lace. Hats were flat and covered with ostrich feathers, shoes had red heels and wide, stiff bows.

French fashion-books presented choices of hairstyles named after famous wearers or after the vision they presented.

à la Fontanges

à la sultane

Dressing gowns were made of Indian cotton imported from Madras by the new East India Company.

à la culebutte

avec des frisons

à l' effrontée

en palissade

The French king's favourite, Mademoiselle de Fontanges, took to wearing her hair held high with ribbons. Frizzy curls went right out of fashion. All the women had their hair piled up on top of their heads. The cheekiest left their ears uncovered so that they could hear the flirtatious remarks whispered to them. Men and women both made use of perfume, make-up, and black silk patches highlighting their cheeks.

The end of the seventeenth century. Rhinegraves disappeared. Coats replaced tunics. Their great advantage was that they had pockets. Some of the more stylish fops wore their cravats tucked into a buttonhole – a fashion adopted from French officers, hurrying to get ready before the battle of Steinkirk, and without the time to tie their cravats.

Wigs that used to flow down in long curls were replaced by wigs that were piled up in pyramids.

Fringes, curls and ribbons everywhere, even on the enormous muffs favoured by men and women alike, marked the new relaxation of the Restoration.

1700

In 1703, a French actress called Madame Dancourt made a great hit in a Roman play, and launched a fashion for a loose, flowing dress, with a belt at the waist. But this *robe volante* was not as simple as it looked – the skirts were held out with hoops of whalebone. The fashion was such a success throughout Europe that extra whaling fleets were sent out to cope with the demand for whalebone.

Men's coats remained waisted, with strips of whalebone stiffening the long skirts. The cuffs were often embroidered or made of brocade of flowered silk. Underneath, waistcoats were still worn long. Everyone powdered their wigs or hair.

In Venice, during the carnival, no-one would go out without a white-painted, lace-edged mask. Women wore a short cape over their dresses. Sometimes doctors wore masks, too, during outbreaks of plague – medicinal herbs tucked into the beaks were supposed to keep away disease.

For indoor wear in Venice, a long waistcoat, a bodice in red and gold brocade, underneath a gown decorated with multicoloured flowers and lined with gold brocade

41

1780

The model farm near the Palace of Versailles where Marie-Antoinette and her ladies would spend afternoons playing dairymaids

Coats and waistcoats both became shorter. White was a popular colour, with spots and stripes also making an appearance.

Queen Marie-Antoinette of France was the most elegant woman in the kingdom. Everything she did was copied immediately.

In French towns, the fashion was for short skirts, which sometimes only went down as far as the ankle, with high waists and the tiny beginnings of a bustle. Huge hats from England completed the outfit.

Men wore three-cornered hats, or sometimes flat, wide-brimmed hats called Pennsylvanians.

A gentleman's cane was as much a part of his dress as his hat or well-powdered wig.

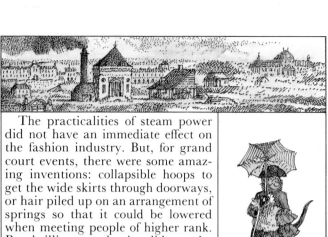

The practicalities of steam power did not have an immediate effect on the fashion industry. But, for grand court events, there were some amazing inventions: collapsible hoops to get the wide skirts through doorways, or hair piled up on an arrangement of springs so that it could be lowered when meeting people of higher rank. But brilliant mechanics did not detract from the lace that foamed at throat and sleeve and hem.

Pets were dressed in perfect miniatures of their owners' clothes.

The law ordained that dancers and actresses had to wear knickers, in case they kicked their skirts too high while on stage. The flounces peeping out from under the petticoat were only lace trimmings to the garters holding up a lady's stockings.

*Coiffure
en qu'es aco*

*Toque galante
au parc anglais*

*Bonnet
à la Voltaire*

A nightcap ensured
that pillows were
kept free of powder.

Hair was no longer cut, but was
piled up on frameworks of wicker and
gauze, with false hair-pieces to pad it
out into all sorts of fantastic shapes.
Flowers, birds, dolls, favourite pets,

Bonnet à la Polichinelle

Pouf à l'Asiatique

Coiffure à la Belle Poule

even vegetables expressed the wearer's personality! When the king was inoculated against smallpox, Marie-Antoinette wore her hair in the shape of the inoculation sponge.

Cartoons made fun of the latest fashion.

45

Everywhere there was change, except for the poor peasants. The United States of America had declared, and won, their independence. The philosopher Rousseau advocated a return to nature. Hygienists recommended giving up wearing whalebone corsets. Everyone seemed to be wanting greater freedom and simplicity in their clothes. As early as 1770 the first mass-produced fashion was put on the market by a French tailor called Dartigalongue. He made suits and dresses in every size and then sold them in the provinces. He even exported them. Ready-to-wear clothing was born!

In Spain, the Duchess of Alba wore the simplest of dresses: a white muslin shift fastened with a belt tied in a huge bow.

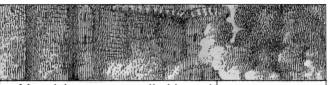

Materials now were all thin and light – muslin, linen, poplin, cottons, tulle, gauze and taffeta. The increasing use of cottons, and the invention of the spinning jenny, greatly promoted the cotton industry in and around Manchester, where the cool damp climate meant that the thread could be spun very fine without breaking.

The upheavals of the French Revolution were felt in radical changes of fashion, too.

The French revolutionaries did not possess the silken breeches, the *culottes*, of the aristocracy.

They wore trousers instead. That is why they were called *sans-culotte*.

A young beau addressing a French republican sporting the new French national colours of red, white and blue

The French revolutionary council prescribed different clothes for different officers of state, and for ordinary citizens too. The tricolour sash is still worn by French officials to this day.

The effects of revolutionary egalitarianism made their way across the Channel, and even seeped into the clubs of St James's. The Prime Minister, Fox, lamented that the more people of fashion adopted a casual manner of dress, the more they broke down the social barriers between them and the working classes and spread dangerous 'levelling and equalizing notions'.

What French citizens were supposed to wear

Government official

The Council of Five Hundred recall more classical times.

Mayor

1790 New ways of dressing popularized the simple and the classical. Women especially wore simple, classical lines and pseudo-Grecian styles.

In menswear, England dominated Europe. This ascendancy was particularly helped by the rise to royal favour of George Brummell, commonly known as Beau Brummell. With the Prince Regent as his protector, Beau Brummell had a great influence, not least on habits of washing, of which he was a great advocate.

For the first time for a long time, men became neat and clean in their appearance.

English dandies and French *incroyables* vied with each other for outrageousness: long puppy-dog locks hung round their ears, their fronts were festooned with medallions, lorgnettes, chains, cameos, their legs decorated with tight trousers or stockings woven in horizontal stripes.

During this period, the change-over from breeches to trousers took place. In 1790, tight-fitting breeches were generally worn either knee-length or ankle-length, with buttons up the outside to knee or thigh level. By 1800, light-coloured trousers were seen. They were tight-fitting, and usually held down with a strap under the instep. When George IV came to the throne in England, he gave a definite lead towards the adoption of trousers for all occasions, and the changeover soon became complete. At the same time, there was a change in footwear from stockings to socks.

Ostrich-feather plume

For women, the high Grecian waistline was accentuated by a ribbon or band under the breasts. Sleeves were short, either in a little puff, or forming a small cap at the shoulder. Legs were either bare or covered with pale stockings.

Extra-modest cap

Short jackets were introduced by Lord Spencer, who cut the tails off his frock-coat so that they did not catch light as he warmed himself in front of the fire.

Pamela-style hat

1830

English inventions, like the railway, and English fashion, led by Beau Brummel, came to the fore. Caped riding-coats, transformed into *redingotes*, swirled into fashion. Everything English was instantly popular.

Women moved their belts back down to their waists. They loved deep layers or jockeys overhanging their sleeves. Running from one side to the other, these were called 'berthas', and were the height of fashion.

The collapsible top-hat solved storage problems

Despite flights of fancy such as that displayed by the French actress, Mademoiselle Mars, when she appeared in her version of a Chinese coolie's dress, middle-class fashion was taking over from aristocratic fantasies. Gradually, skirts became longer and fuller, corsets and stiffening started to reappear.

Belt buckles and bracelets were in locket and medallion form, inside which you could hide a portrait of your beloved. Jewellery started to have sentimental value.

Hair piled on top and fastened with a Spanish comb displayed the charms of a long, white neck.

53

The art
of tying
a cravat

At this time, when the Western world was at its peak, extending its influence to the farthest corners of the earth, an important question began to be posed: if trousers could be held up by braces over the shoulders, what was going to happen to a gentleman's shape? The abolition of knee breeches had led to the disappearance of garters, and now there were no belts to mark the waist. But, happily, there still remained the cravat, the stylish tying of which could (with your valet's help) take over an hour, and which was the true mark of the gentleman.

Women's clothing changed little: the face framed with ringlets, the body with full, layered skirts.

Novelties:
overcoats and
checked trousers

Princess de Metternich was the most elegant woman at the court of Napoleon III. She was impressed by the drawings of an English dressmaker, Charles Frederick Worth, who had set up a workroom in the rue de la Paix. Paris fashion designers had been launched.

The characteristic dress of the age was the crinoline, which swung and swirled to the elegant waltzes of the time. At first, it was simply an underskirt stiffened with horsehair, but it soon developed into a metal cage supporting fourteen metres of cloth.

Fitting a new dress

Underskirt and afternoon gown

In the new world of America, all sorts of inventions were overturning the old order. One was blue jeans.

A demonstration in San Francisco proved the strength of Oscar Levi-Strauss' new denim jeans.

Back in Europe, outdoor life took on greater attractions, although sea-bathing was rather more an excuse for wearing the latest elegant fantasy than for indulging in sport.

In this changing world, crinolines gave way to the bustle, a half-circle of whalebone holding out the skirts behind.

Bustles caused a sensation when the fashionable first appeared in them at race-meetings and evening parties. Worth said he got the idea from seeing a street-sweeper with her skirts tucked up behind.

Dress gloves

Women had morning clothes, afternoon clothes and evening dresses. Afternoon visits were made in heavy cloth, but evening-wear was light, the bustle smaller, with a long, lacy train which could be twirled and twitched flirtatiously.

Gentlemen's evening dress: a black tail-coat and grey striped trousers.

Rubber was not only useful for braces.

With the help of straps,

it could be used to correct all sorts of natural lacks.

A cartoonist's view of fashion.

Dressing and undressing followed a logical sequence. After a quick wash . . .

Over the corset, an underbodice. Then the careful lacing-on of the bustle.

The corset was the heart of women's clothing. It served both as a support for their supposedly fragile bodies, and as a way of emphasizing their figures.

It could only be put on with the help of a lady's maid.

... the corset was laced over the chemise.
Then came stockings and pantaloons.

A shagreen handbag
and silk ribbons. The
beautiful and the
useful.

A few skirts to flounce everything out, and
finally a neat little dress for morning visits.

Shoes were worn only
in the house. For out-
door wear: tightly-
laced boots to display
the
ankle.

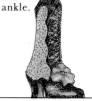

The invention of 'lazy maid's' lacing
made it possible for women to dress
themselves.

Corsets were controversial. Accord-
ing to the doctors, four-fifths of heart
attacks in women were caused by their
corsets having been laced too tightly.

1900

Bloomers
revolutionized
women's casual wear.

Cycling and motor-car driving along dusty country roads called for long coats and veils.

Even on foot, gentlemen wore long, fur-collared coats and highly polished silk top hats.

Women gave up the bustle. Skirts hugged the hips and widened out down to the ground. Necklines rose right up to the chin and sleeves swelled into legs-o'-mutton.

Hats became enormous.

For the first time, fur coats became fashionable. Instead of being simply a lining, the fur was a feature.

But the real revolution came from Paul Poiret, popularized in England by the hugely successful Liberty's. Without a corset, dresses hung straight down, with just a ribbon underneath the breasts to give a little shape. In a few years, women's clothes had gone from weighing 3 kilogrammes to weighing only about 900 grammes.

Getting on and off trams meant that women's skirts had to get shorter.

Soldiers coming back from the First World War hardly recognized their wives, with their flat figures and their hair bobbed short.

People danced lively dances like the Charleston or the tango. Skirts got shorter and shorter. Suspender belts took over from corsets. For men, evening-wear moved from the frock-coat and striped trousers to the dinner-jacketed evening suit.

1920

1936

The big steamships made travel between Europe and America easy and fashionable. Trends were set by Hollywood stars, although rich American women still preferred to do their shopping among the fashion-houses of Paris.

One-piece swimsuits and bathing caps were really designed to swim in.

Plus-fours, tweed jackets and flat caps were highly fashionable, with the dashing Prince of Wales leading the way.

Joan Crawford set the fashion for little hats tilted over one eye. Robert Taylor began the trend for Prince of Wales checks and vicuna overcoats.

1940

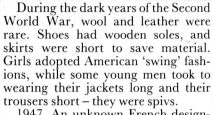

During the dark years of the Second World War, wool and leather were rare. Shoes had wooden soles, and skirts were short to save material. Girls adopted American 'swing' fashions, while some young men took to wearing their jackets long and their trousers short – they were spivs.

1947. An unknown French designer, Christian Dior, created a revolution: gone was the time of austerity; here were full, flowing lines, tight waists, generous hips. The American newspapers called it the New Look.

Betty Grable: the first pin-up girl, and darling of the American forces

The New Look swept the world. Women who couldn't afford new dresses let down their skirts and tacked capes and hems of fur on to their jackets. It was the golden age of Balmain, Fath and Balenciaga. When Chanel brought out her neat, braid-trimmed suit, it was copied by a whole generation of women.

Other novelties were the duffle-coat, made over from coats worn by soldiers during the war, and scooters, which girls could ride without snagging their new nylon stockings.

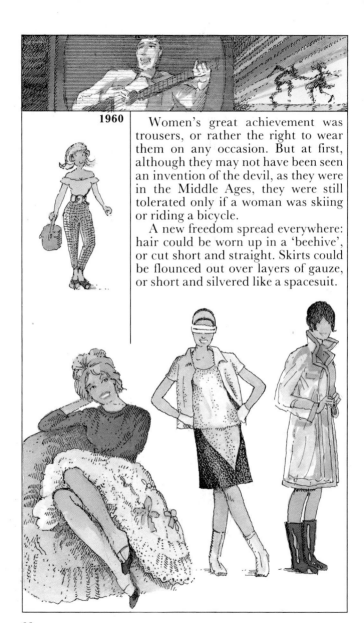

1960

Women's great achievement was trousers, or rather the right to wear them on any occasion. But at first, although they may not have been seen an invention of the devil, as they were in the Middle Ages, they were still tolerated only if a woman was skiing or riding a bicycle.

A new freedom spread everywhere: hair could be worn up in a 'beehive', or cut short and straight. Skirts could be flounced out over layers of gauze, or short and silvered like a spacesuit.

Suddenly, men grew their hair longer and their trousers widened out into bell-bottoms. At the same time, women went wild for mini-skirts, mini-dresses, mini-coats. New technology made it possible to weave clinging nylon tights, while boots got longer and longer until they reached mid-thigh.

Hippies preferred trailing shawls, coats made from Afghan goatskin, floppy hats and headbands.

The Beatles, with their clean, frank faces and pudding-basin haircuts, made long hair safe.

1970

When the old French cotton weave *de Nîmes* came back to Europe from America as denim, made up into jeans, jackets and dungarees, the two sexes were able to dress identically, swapping tee-shirts, bomber jackets and trainers.

Women could now wear men's jackets, waistcoats and shirts. Men's suits were simpler and more casual.

Never had trends and choices been so wide and varied.

Japanese, Dutch, Italian, American, British and often French, designers can come from almost anywhere in the world.

You can wear your hair in a lion's mane, in a crew-cut, in an orange and green Mohican. You can wear a baseball jacket or a long coat, a mini-skirt or a full-length dress, white shoes, grey shoes, flat or pointed or on stiletto heels, futuristic or old-fashioned . . .

You can wear anything at all, except, of course, last year's fashions.

An A to Z of Fashion

Accessories
Anything that isn't the actual garment – hats, shoes, scarves, bags, belts, jewellery.

Accordion pleating
Very popular in the middle of the nineteenth century. Skirts became extremely complicated, with the over-skirt fastened back and up and the lower parts of the legs covered by an under-skirt. The picture was completed by a full draped bustle over which the fabric fell in a long train. Fringes, ruches and pleats decorated every edge.

Aiguillettes
Decorative metal tags for the ends of the laces or points which attached hose to belts, or, in the Tudor period, almost anything to almost anything else.

Antimacassars
Cloths over the backs of chairs to protect the furniture from hair oil. Particularly popular in the late 19th century.

Baldric
Plantagenet decorative sash, often brightly coloured and hung with bells.

Bathing costume
In Victorian times, these were usually knee-length, with short sleeves. They were dark, and decorated with braid and lace.

Bikini
A different kind of bathing costume. The effect when it was first worn in 1946 was supposed to have been as explosive as the recent explosion of an atom bomb on Bikini Atoll.

Bloomers
A species of long knickerbocker invented by the American Amelia Bloomer. She hoped that they would replace the crinoline, but fashion prevailed over practicality.

Boa
Long, floating scarf made of ostrich feathers, highly popular among women at the turn of the century.

Buskin
Greek boots worn by men.

Camiknickers
Invented in the 1920s, their scantiness and the pastel shades contrasted with the underwear of previous decades.

Chemise
Silk or linen undershirt.

Chin-cloth
Cloth draped round neck and shoulders by Persian dignitaries.

Cloche hat
1920s woman's hat shaped like a bell (hence the name, from the French for bell), which came down over the ears to cover the short, bobbed hair, and emphasized the new boyish lines of the New Woman.

Corsets
Even in the 12th century, a light corset of leather was thought necessary to show off women's figures under their close-fitting gowns. By the 16th century, both men and women were prepared to wear corsets of metal, padded with soft leather against the skin, to give them the desired long-bodied, flat-stomached silhouette. Even the simplicity and freedom of Dior's New Look depended on a corset to hold in the waist to the tiny dimensions demanded by the designer. Corsets emphasized men's idealized view of women, with a slender waist and flat stomach, the bust thrust forward and the hips pushed out.

Cravat
Took over from the ruff and neckerchief as neck-wear for gentlemen in the 17th century. Said to have got its name from the Croat guard employed by the French Louis XIV who introduced its wear to the fashionable courts of Europe.

Crinoline
Originally a fabric made of horse-hair (from the French *crin*, meaning horse's mane), it came to mean the stiff, hooped, huge petticoats which held out ladies' skirts in Victorian times.

Damask
A form of weaving first worked out in the town of Damask in Syria.

Domino
A shortening of the Latin *Benedicamus domino*, 'Let us pray to the Lord', this was the cowl and robe worn by priests in the Middle Ages. Became a costume to wear to a masked ball.

Embroidery
From the earliest Egyptian clothing through to contemporary evening-wear and bridal gowns, patterns sewn on to cloth has been one of the easiest and most effective forms of decoration. Many countries and regions have their own distinctive patterns which they use for embroidery.

English gown
A simple satin gown with elbow-length sleeves ending in ruffles or a large puff, and a low round neck, worn in the mid-18th century.

Farthingale
Introduced to England by Henry VIII's first wife,

the Spanish Catherine of Aragon. Whalebone hoops were inserted horizontally at equal intervals down the petticoat, increasing in diameter from waist to ground, so that a cone-shaped or bell-shaped silhouette was achieved. Several ordinary petticoats were worn on top of the farthingale to hide the whalebone bands.

Gainsborough hat
As wigs became smaller in the mid-18th century, hats and bonnets became more popular. Among the most fashionable were the huge picture hats, decorated with ostrich plumes and ribbons, and named after the painter who made them famous.

Gaiters
Popular in the eighteenth century to protect the bottoms of the new ankle-length trousers, these

were made of thick cloth and could be buttoned over the tops of the shoes and round the ankles.

Galoshes
Rubber overshoes to protect leather shoes and boots from the mud of unmade-up roads.

Garters
A band worn round the knee or thigh to keep up the stockings or socks. Made famous in England by Edward III, who saved a lady from embarrassment at a court ball when her garter slipped from her leg to the floor. Picking it up, he declared 'Honi soit qui mal y pense' (Shame to him who thinks ill of it), placed the garter on his arm, and founded the Order of the Garter, the noblest order of English chivalry.

Haik
Light transparent cloth, very finely pleated, worn by the pharaoh of Ancient Egypt and his queen.

Hedgehog wig
A woolly style of wig introduced to England from France in the 1770s.

Inverness coat
Mid-Victorian travelling coat, usually made of plaid or checked cloth, it reached to mid-calf, topped by a shoulder cape and soft collar. The whole was fastened round the waist with a belt.

Jacket
Originally the ordinary clothing of the peasants, Jack being a common name amongst the working people, it persists as one of the most practical clothes ever invented.

Jockey boot
Very popular after 1816, a short boot with a turned-down cuff of buff or yellow leather.

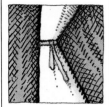

Kilt
Length of woven plaid cloth pleated and wrapped round the waist to hang to mid-calf. Scottish male national dress.

Kimono
Japanese long-sleeved gown wrapped round the body and fastened with a wide belt.

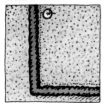

Lampshade skirt
One of the narrow-hemmed absurdities with which fashionable women used to handicap themselves between 1910 and 1914.

The First World War enforced a new practicality.

Macaroni
Late eighteenth-century English term for a dandy. Used mockingly by English troops towards the American rebels during the War of Independence in the song 'Yankee Doodle Dandy', where Yankee Doodle stuck a feather in his cap and thought himself fashionable, a macaroni. After the Yankees beat the English, though, they used 'Yankee Doodle Dandy' as a proud marching-song.

Mao suit
High-collared, buttoned suit worn by men and women alike during the 1960s in China. Named after the leader of China, Chairman Mao Dze Dhong.

Monocle
A corrective lens for one eye worn by men about 100 years ago

as a symbol of their importance and authority.

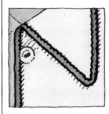

Necklaces
In the early 1930s, necklaces were worn long, hanging below the waist and knotted there. The reaction by the late 1930s was expressed in chokers worn tightly round the neck.

Obi
Wide silk belt worn over the Japanese kimono.

Over-tunic
Similar to the close-fitting, long-sleeved doublet, but longer, and with a skirt attached. Worn in the 15th century.

Panama hat
Wide-brimmed hat popular at the turn of the century, and made, when it was first invented, from a single leaf of the Central American screw-pine tree.

Parasol
Umbrella used to protect the carrier against the effects of sunshine from the 17th century onwards It didn't do for people of fashion to have tanned skin like the peasants who worked in the fields.

Patch box
In the early 18th century, cosmetics came to be used more heavily than ever, to hide the effects of the white powder from wigs drifting down on to the wearer's face. Both men and women used small black spots or patches to mark what they felt was their most beautiful feature, cheek, or mouth, or eye. Patch boxes and cosmetic cases were worn about the person.

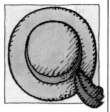

Queen's bird head-dress
Worn in Ancient Egypt, it was a cap in the form of a bird's wing and tail, with a vulture's head over the forehead.

Quilting
Two cloths with padding in between sewn together in patterns for warmth and decoration. Popular in Jacobean times as a defence against daggers.

Reticule
A small purse or pouch. In the 12th century these were made of silk or leather and worn by women, hanging from their belts. In the 19th century, a velvet or bead-embroidered reticule was an essential part of

formal day-wear, carried clasped in the hand.

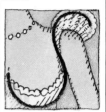

Slashes
A form of decoration popular in the 15th century, where rich cloth had holes cut in it so that the cloth underneath could be seen peeping through. Sleeve slashes were often fastened with aiguillettes.

Stetson
American cowboy hat defined by its volume, the biggest being a ten-gallon hat.

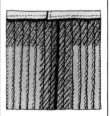

Tail-coat
This first made its appearance in the early 1780s. It had a very deep, turned-down collar reaching to the ears, and the skirts of the coat

cut away in front so that they hung down in a tail behind.

Ulster
Long winter overcoat shaped like a dressing-gown. First invented in Ireland in the 19th century.

Unisex
Clothes which can be worn equally well by either sex, like the ubiquitous blue jeans.

Underwear
Worn sporadically, and in greater and lesser quantities, from the early Persians onwards. The invention of nylon has revolutionized the design of underwear in the twentieth century.

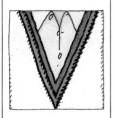

Vandyke collar
Lace-edged collar popular in the early 17th century and named after the famous court painter, Sir Anthony Van Dyck.

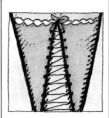

Wellington boot
Named after the Duke of Wellington, the Wellington boot started its career in the 1830s as a plain, high leather boot. The invention of moulded rubber transformed it into the impermeable article we know today.

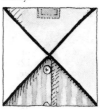

Xeranthemum
One of the plants more commonly called 'everlastings' or *immortelles*, which can be dried.

Xystis
Long tunic worn by charioteers in Ancient Greece.

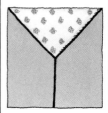

Yashmak
Veil worn by Muslim women to cover the mouth and nose.

Yelek
Long tunic worn by Egyptian women.

Yoke
Portion of bodice which covers the shoulders. In the 15th century this was often highlighted by being made of different-coloured cloth.

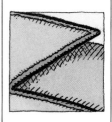

Zip fastener
1893: perhaps the most significant invention in clothing since early man first thought of the button.

What the Author Saw

Like anybody interested in clothes, Jean-Louis Besson has been fascinated by the kinds of clothes depicted in old paintings, sculptures and engravings. In his illustrations to this book, he has sometimes drawn inspiration from the pictures he has seen. Perhaps you may recognize them from museums and books:

Abraham Bosse, Van Dyck, title page; Coptic portrait, p.15; frescoes from Manta Castle, p.23; Boccaccio's Wedding, by Adimari, p.25; Carpaccio, Giovanni Bellini, Francesco del Cossa, p.26; Balthazar Estrense, Pisanello, Roger van der Weyden, Petrus Christus, the Master of the Legend of St Madeleine, p.27; Hans Holbein, p.28; Titian, p.29; Crispin de Passe, Caulery, p.31; Sandvoort, John Tradescant, Van Dyck, p.32; Abraham Bosse, Daniel Mytens, p.33; Velasquez, Lebrun, Teniers, pp.36-37; Watteau, J.F. de Troy, p.40; Ghislandi, Pietro Longhi, p.41; Moreau the Younger, p.43; Goya, p.46; Carle Vernet, p.49; Gérard, Prud'hon, Rouget, p.50; Devéria, p.52; Mussini, p.53; Baron de l'Empesé, p.54; Jean Beraud, p.57; T.T. Heine, p.60; G. Barbier, p.61; André Marty, p.62.

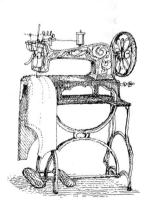

Also available in the *Discoverers* **series:**

The companion volume in this 2-volume history of costume:

Uniforms Through the Ages

Books about Nature:
Spring
Summer
Autumn
Winter
Your Cat
Flowers
The Book of Rivers

Books about Science:
The Book of the Sky

Books about History:
Ships and Seafarers
Painting and Painters
The Book of Inventions and Discoveries